Samuel Alexander Harrison

Wenlock Christison and the Early Friends in Talbot County, Maryland

A Paper Read before the Maryland Historical Society, March 9th, 1874

Samuel Alexander Harrison

Wenlock Christison and the Early Friends in Talbot County, Maryland
A Paper Read before the Maryland Historical Society, March 9th, 1874

ISBN/EAN: 9783337165666

Printed in Europe, USA, Canada, Australia, Japan

Cover: Foto ©ninafisch / pixelio.de

More available books at **www.hansebooks.com**

Fund-Publication, No. 12.

WENLOCK CHRISTISON,

AND THE

EARLY FRIENDS

IN

Talbot County, Maryland:

A Paper read before the Maryland Historical Society,

March 9th, 1874.

BY

SAMUEL A. HARRISON, M. D.

Baltimore, 1878.

PEABODY PUBLICATION FUND.

COMMITTEE ON PUBLICATION.

1877–8.

HENRY STOCKBRIDGE.
E. J. D. CROSS,
JOHN W. M. LEE.

PRINTED BY JOHN MURPHY,
PRINTER TO THE MARYLAND HISTORICAL SOCIETY,
BALTIMORE, 1878.

PREFACE.

THE paper which follows was originally written as a contribution to a projected History of Talbot county, Maryland. This will account for and perhaps excuse the introduction of so many references to persons, places and events which must possess merely a local interest. These could not have been eliminated from the memoir, when it was to be presented through the Historical Society to a wider public than that for which it was designed, without recasting the whole and rejecting what some may think gives to it its chief value.

The engrafting upon the narrative of the life of the Quaker confessor so much that is purely incidental, relating to the early Friends, renders the essay liable to unfavorable criticism as a symmetrical literary work; but a correction of this very evident fault might, also, impair its value, while it rendered it more artistic. Besides, such correction would be directly contrary to the wishes of the Historical Society as expressed at the time of the reading of the paper.

Whatever claims to originality the memoir possesses are based upon that portion which relates to Wenlock Christison's career as a citizen of Maryland, in Talbot county. Of that part of his life which was spent in New England, and which indeed is the most interesting, the writer of this essay has done little more than glean the incidents scattered here and there in a rather rare and confusedly written book, and arrange them in some kind of order—a task by no means the most easy of accomplishment.

But what has been related of the life of this worthy in Maryland, has been derived, in great measure, from sources hitherto unexamined, or at least not examined for the purposes for which they are now used.

This memoir makes no pretensions to completeness; for of the subject all that remains are a few historical *exuviæ*, from which the paleontological biographer must vainly try to restore the form and features of a man deeply buried in the drift of centuries

S. A. H

WOODSTOCK, *August 1, 1877.*

WENLOCK CHRISTISON.

Gentlemen of the
   Maryland Historical Society:

IT should have been made one of the conditions precedent to the acceptance of your invitation to read a paper before your body, that you should be content to receive, in lieu of an important contribution to the history of the State, an insignificant addition to the annals of a county. Whatever might have been expected of me, this last is all that I could have honestly promised. It would be sheer pretension to claim for the researches which I have been engaged in making the importance that attaches to investigations into the transactions of great nations, or into the lives of those distinguished personages who have illustrated their country's history. On the other hand it would be an affectation of humility to disclaim the value of local annals and memoirs of local celebrities for the proper understanding of the true story of the greater state, or to ascend higher, for the proper comprehension of a true philosophy of general history. The limits which a sense of my own insufficiency for a nobler task has set to my labors in the field of historic research, are the boundaries of my own native county of Talbot. Beyond them I have not ventured to step. I have thought that if I could suitably note down the simple events that have transpired within her bounds, or rescue from entire oblivion the memories of her almost forgotten worthies, I should be doing no mean work, though humble, but should be aiding in elucidating the yet unwritten story of the State itself, and be in some appreciable degree helping him who, though longed for, is yet to come, the Historian of Maryland.

The chief resources of the annalist for the earlier years of Talbot County, are the Court Records in the offices of the Clerk and the Register of Wills; the registries of the several parishes embraced within the county limits, now in the possession of the Vestries of the churches; and finally, the minutes of the Friends' meetings, held at and near the head of Third Haven creek, which are now in the custody of James Dixon, a most worthy representative of that most excellent religious society. Of these records, those belonging to the county, extending back to its very organization in 1661 or 2, are in a singularly good state of preservation. Those belonging to the vestries of

St. Michael's and St. Peter's parishes—those of St. Paul's not having been particularly examined, that parish having been mostly in Queen Anne's County —are more incomplete, but still exceedingly valuable. Those belonging to the Third Haven meeting of Friends are in a perfect state of preservation, and but for an hiatus here and there, owing to the carelessness of the clerks of the meeting, would be complete from the year 1676 to the present time. These are most precious documents, and are as interesting to the local annalist as the Grecian Iliad is to the classic historian, or the Scandinavian Eddas to the northern antiquary.[1] In examining our earliest court records, what was my astonishment, to find the name of a man, as party of the second part to a deed of gift, who, in connection with the Quaker persecutions in Massachusetts, is mentioned in all the histories of New England. This astonishment was increased when the minutes of the Friends' meetings came under examination, and it was learned that this man was a permanent resident of Talbot County, and that at his house the very first meeting of Friends, of which there is any official record, ever held in the county, in

---

[1] As an evidence of the estimate that is placed upon these minutes of the Friends' Meeting at Third Haven, and as a matter worthy of record, it may be stated that the Historical Society of Pennsylvania has had a full and complete copy of them made and deposited among its archives. It may be mentioned too, without impropriety, that the writer of this memoir has made an abstract of these minutes, by which, in case of their destruction, they could be restored in all essential particulars.

the State, or perhaps in the whole country, assembled. Of this man, Wenlock Christison, it is proposed to give an account, more full and complete than has been done by any one hitherto.

The persecutions of the Quakers by the authorities, civil and ecclesiastical, of New England, have long afforded a favorite theme for the animadversions of two classes of people, the bigotedly pious, and the narrowly patriotic—of those whose religion serves them as much for the reprehension of the conduct of others as for the rectification of their own, and of those whose patriotism, limited by state lines, prefers to indulge sectional antipathies and prejudices, rather than a comprehensive love of a common country. Now, these persecutions by men who had left their own homes to find in the wilderness "freedom to worship God," were certainly a sad and mortifying exhibition. They are deserving of our condemnation, but this condemnation will have mitigation from a remembrance that these atrocities were not peculiar to New England, but that George Fox was imprisoned and whipped, and that Ann Downer was beaten in Old England before William Leddra and Mary Dyer were hung in Boston. In America, Round Head and Cavalier, Massachusetts and Virginia united in these persecutions; and even Maryland, with her noble charter of religious toleration, of which we are so proud, has not wholly escaped the foul blot. The laws of Virginia against these people were almost as severe as those of Plymouth or Boston, though they certainly were not enforced with nearly so much rigor:[1] and we of Maryland must blush to read that the Council proceedings of the 23d of July, 1659, contain an order directing all "Justices of the Peace to seize any Quakers that might come into their districts, and whip them from constable to constable until they should reach the bounds of the Province." It is not absolutely certain that any Quaker was ever whipped in Maryland, though one historian of the Society states that three were fined for extending hospitality to one of the preachers who had been ordered to leave the province, and that another was whipped for refusing to assist the Sheriff in arresting the same preacher, who, after his arrest was imprisoned a year and a day, and was then sent away to New England, whence he

[1] According to an Act of the Assembly of Burgesses of Virginia, passed in 1663, Quakers who should " assemble themselves together to the number of five or more, of the age of sixteen years and upwards, under pretence of joining in religious worship, not authorized in England or this country," were fined 200 lbs. of tobacco for the first offence, 500 lbs. for the second, and for the third they were banished from the colony. Ship masters bringing Quakers into the colony after July 1st, of that year, were to be fined 5,000 lbs. of tobacco, and enjoined to carry them out again. A person entertaining a Quaker "in or near his house to Preach or Teach," was fined 5,000 lbs. of tobacco for every offence. One-half of these fines were to go to the informer, and one-half to the parish vestries for "pious uses."—*An Abridgement of the Laws in Force and Use in Her Majesty's Plantations.* . . . . London, John Nicholson, 1704, demi 8o.

returned to Maryland again, to give much trouble, not only to the civil authorities but to his own friends the Quakers, by whom he was finally "disowned." There were a few cases of fines, imprisonment and banishment, beside those of Thomas Thurston, and those who gave him hospitality and refused to assist the Sheriff in his arrest.[1] Accepting these instances as veritable, there are no others in our State Records of any corporal punishment having been inflicted upon any Quaker—no mutilation by "cutting off the ears," or "branding in the hand"—no instance of the barbarity of being "tied to a great gun," flogged through the town and turned adrift in the woods—no instance of being hanged by the neck until dead, followed by stripping of the body and refusal of decent burial—such as occurred in New England. It is very gratifying to know that after a very short interval of the predominance in the province of a spirit of intolerance towards these people, Maryland assumed her early sentiment of freedom of worship, and that she who was from the first the refuge of the persecuted, became the sanctuary of the religiously proscribed, and as such, of the Friends. From a libertine King, a papistical Proprietary, and a prelatical Assembly, these people received an indulgence not vouchsafed by a sanctimonious

---

[1] Norris' *Early Friends in Maryland.*

Protector, by an evangelical Governor and by a General Court, one of the qualifications for a seat in which was church membership.[1] Our books of laws indicate, and authentic history records that our provincial authorities after a short period of persecution, which at the worst was more irritating than cruel, became not simply tolerant, but solicitous to protect the Friends in

[1] There is a remarkable confirmation of the statement that the government of Maryland was very liberal towards even the Quakers, who were persecuted by almost every community where they appeared, which has not been before noticed. There appears to have been a small society or settlement of Friends—a settlement of which the historians of that body of Christians have failed to give any account whatever—within the territory disputed by Virginia and Maryland, upon the borders of Somerset and Accomack counties. An attempt was made by one Col. Scarborough or Scarburgh, to bring these people under the jurisdiction of Virginia. But they positively refused to acknowledge the authority of that province and claimed to be under the government of the Lord Proprietary of Maryland. This was in 1663. It would appear that anteriorly some of these people had removed out of Accomack, into what they supposed was Lord Baltimore's territory, and having accepted patents from under his seal, they persisted in regarding themselves inhabitants of Maryland, notwithstanding Col. Scarborough's threats of violence. But more singular than this, some of the Commissioners appointed by the Governor and Council of Maryland for the granting of land titles—for this was before the organization of Somerset county—were Quakers. In a commission appointed in 1665, composed of seven persons, no less than three were of the society of Friends, viz: *Stephen Horsey*, who had once been a burgess in the Virginia Assembly, *George Johnson* and *Henry Boston*. The recalcitrant Quakers mentioned in the report of Col. Scarborough to the Virginia Assembly, from which this account is taken, were *Thomas Price* and *Ambrose Dixon*. They and their associates were all settled along the Annemessex. Col. Scarborough's description of these people is exceedingly curious, and anything but flattering, but it doubtless reflects the sentiments concerning them prevailing at the time. When Somerset was organized in 1666, there were three Quakers acting as land commissioners, and probably as Justices of the Peace. All this serves to indicate with what feelings they were regarded by the proprietary government of Maryland.—*Accomack County, Virginia Records.*

all their rights and privileges, even so far as to modify the statutes as if, as it were, to humor their peculiarities. Nay more, it will be seen in the sequel that Quakers were allowed to take seats in the General Assembly of the province, as legislators, at a time when elsewhere they were suffering proscription, if not actual persecution—if indeed proscription be not the worst persecution. To be sure, the property of Friends who would not "train with the militia," or who would not contribute to the support of war by either personal service or by the payment of taxes, or who would not pay the assessment of church rates for the maintenance of "hireling priests," and for the building or repairing of "worship houses," as the clergy and churches of the establishment were called in ignominy, was seized and sold by the Sheriffs, and so continued to be for many years, down to a comparatively recent date, as their records of sufferings attest: but they were exempt from personal violence and insult, they were protected in their modes and places of worship, they had concessions granted to their conscientious scruples, and they had deference shown to their peculiarities, by statutes passed in their behalf.

A very thorough examination of the Records of the Court of Talbot County, and an equally thorough examination of the "minutes" of the meetings of Friends, at Third Haven, have revealed not a single instance of personal violence inflicted in that county upon a Quaker on account of his religion; and it is to be noted that our Court Records extend back to 1662, a period when persecution was rife elsewhere, and that the minutes of the meetings commence in 1676, a period when Friends were still emulous of martyrdom, and would have been sure to record any case of "suffering." Incidentally it may be mentioned here, that the only instances of persecution, or seeming persecution, in all the annals of Talbot County, are the *disbarring* of one John Walker, an attorney, in 1689, on account of his being a Roman Catholic, and of his refusal to take oaths of "supremacy and abhorrency;" and the arrest and imprisonment in the Easton jail of *Joseph Hartley*, a Methodist preacher, in 1779, on the "charge of preaching and teaching the gospel contrary to an Act of Assembly, entitled 'An Act for the better security of the State'"—to make use of the very words of his recognizance, as recorded in the proceedings of the Court. But in both these instances political rather than religious intolerance was the motive of the laws under which the persons named were punished; and it will be observed they both occurred at periods of revolution—the one at or about the time of the accession of William and Mary to the throne of

England, and the other at or about the time of the overthrow of British rule in the united colonies.[1]

There are reasons to believe, at least there are some circumstances to render it highly probable, that Maryland and Talbot County itself, where, almost from the first foundation of Quakerism in America, there was a society of Friends near the head of Third Haven Creek, afforded an asylum for many of the persecuted and harassed Friends of Old England, New England, New York, Virginia, and other colonies. There have been families in this county, the representatives of which bore the names—christian or surname, or both —of some of the very earliest and most prominent, prominent for labor and suffering, of the Friends; and these families, as far as we have evidence, were of this society of religious people.

[1] What is here said of the absence from Maryland of religious intolerance, must not be understood to mean there were no religious disabilities in that province. The existence of a State church or 'establishment' necessarily involves the religious disabilities of all dissenters. The Church of England was made the established church of the province in 1692, or more completely in 1702. From the very first, the Quakers of Talbot protested against paying the 40 lbs of tobacco per poll for the support of the "idolatrous priests," as they called the clergy, and the further assessment for building their " worship houses," as the churches were opprobriously called in a region where they possessed no steeples, and could not be called "steeple houses" as in New and Old England.

It is proper to say, as a matter of simple history, and not by way of reflecting upon the people of any sect or section, that when the intolerant laws of Virginia and Maryland were in operation, the Puritans were either dominant in those provinces, or their spirit was largely influential in legislation and in society.

Thus, there was living in Talbot, anterior to 1726, when he died, a certain *John Burneyeat*. Among the very earliest of the Friends was John Edmondson, a wealthy trader, who entertained George Fox, in 1672. One *Josias Crouch*, gave, for a while, his name to the island in the mouth of Wye river. *Thomas Taylor* was the first clerk of the meeting at Third Haven, as early as 1676. Now, to those who are familiar with Quaker hagiology, these names are suggestive of those belonging to the most conspicuous of the departed saints and confessors of the times of trial. Doubtless there are or were representatives in this county of other more obscure but not less holy personages, who sought and found a sanctuary within the bounds of Talbot. But without resorting to conjecture, there is one well authenticated instance of a person who suffered much persecution for his profession and practice as a Quaker, and who, after being beaten, imprisoned, banished and even condemned to death, came to Talbot, here settled, married, rose to distinction, and died. This man was that Wenlock Christison, already mentioned, who figured so conspicuously during those trials in Boston which resulted in the execution of four persons, and in the whipping, imprisoning and banishment of many others "barely for being such as were called Quakers," to use the very words of *George Bishope*, who has most fully reported these trials in his book entitled *New England Judged*.[1] This book constitutes one of the most terrible indictments ever framed against any people, and though written by a Quaker—by one of those with whose character we are accustomed to associate all that is gentle and mild—it must be regarded as being as vengeful in spirit as it is ferocious in language, as the title pages, alone, sufficiently indicate. George Bishope having been one of the sufferers at the hands of the authorities of Massachusetts, much may be pardoned to him. Among those who endured the persecution, of which this book gives account, Wenlock Christison was not the least conspicuous. No account has reached us of the origin of this much suffering and brave man. His name, which is written by some of the New-England historians, Christopherson, (and in the Talbot records, Cristison,) is thought to have a Scotch derivation; and the sturdy character of him who bore it inclines one to the belief that in him flowed the blood of the Covenanters. He uniformly claimed to be a British subject, and not amenable to the colonial authorities. In one place he is represented to have said that he came out of England. The first notice that is given of him

[1] Of this rather rare and exceedingly curious book, a copy of which the writer was enabled to use through the courtesy of the Cherry Street (Philadelphia) Monthly Meeting of Friends, the following are the grimly quaint titles of the first and second parts:

New-England Judged,
BY THE
Spirit of the Lord.

In Two Parts.

First, Containing a Brief Relation of the Sufferings of the People call'd Quakers in *New-England*, from the Time of their first Arrival there, in the Year 1656, to the Year 1660. Wherein their Merciless Whippings, Chainings, Finings, Imprisonings, Starvings, Burning in the Hand, Cutting off Ears, and Putting to Death, with divers other Cruelties, inflicted upon the Bodies of Innocent Men and Women, only for Conscience-sake, are briefly described. In Answer to the Declaration of their Persecutors Apologizing for the same, MDCLIX,

Second Part, Being a farther Relation of the Cruel and Bloody Sufferings of the People call'd Quakers in *New-England*, Continued from *anno* 1660, to *anno* 1665. Beginning with the Sufferings of *William Leddra*, whom they put to Death.

Formerly Published by **George Bishop**, and now somewhat Abreviated.

With an Appendix,

Containing the Writings of several of the Sufferers; with some Notes, shewing the Accomplishment of their Prophecies; and a Postscript of the Judgments of God, that have befallen divers of their Persecutors.

ALSO,

An Answer to *Cotton Mather's* Abuses of the said People, in his late History of *New-England*, Printed *anno* 1702. The whole being at this time Published in the said Peoples Vindication, as a Reply to all his Slanderous Calumnies.

And they overcame by the Blood of the Lamb, and by the word of their Testimony; and they loved not their Lives unto the Death, Rev. 12. 11.

LONDON, Printed and Sold by *T. Sowle,* in *White-Hart-Court* in *Gracious-Street.* 1703.

New England judged.

The Second Part.

BEING,

A RELATION of the Cruel and Bloody Sufferings of the People called *QUAKERS*, in the Jurisdiction, chiefly, of the *Massachusets;* beginning with the Sufferings of *William Leddra,* whom they Murthered, and Hung upon a Tree, at *Boston,* the 14th of the first Month, 166$^0_1$. barely for being such a one as is called a *Quaker,* and coming within their Jurisdiction; and ending with the Sufferings of *Edward Wharton,* the 3d Month, 1665. and the remarkable Judgments of God, in the Death of *John Endicot,* Governour, *John Norton,* High Priest, and *Humphry Adderton,* Major-General.

By *George Bishope.*

(Somewhat abbreviated, as the former.)

Fill ye up then the measure of your Fathers; ye Serpents, ye Generation of Vipers, How can ye escape the Damnation of Hell?
Wherefore, behold, I send unto you Prophets, and wise Men, and Scribes, and some of them ye shall Kill and Crucifie; and some of them shall you Scourge in your Synagogues, and Persecute from City to City.
That upon you may come all the Righteous Blood shed upon the Earth, from the Blood of Righteous Abel, *unto the Blood of* Zacharias, *Son of* Barachias, *whom ye slew between the Temple and the Altar.*
Verily, I say unto you, All these things shall come on this Generation, Mat. 23, 32, 33, 34, 35, 36.

London, Printed and Sold by **T. Sowle,** in *White-Hart-Court,* in *Gracious-Street,* 1702.

in Bishope's book is that of his being, with many others of the Friends, in prison in Boston on the 13th of the 10th month, (December,) 1660. Among these prisoners was William Leddra, who was destined to suffer death by hanging for his profession. It would appear that Wenlock Christison had no settled home at this time, but was wandering from place to place, engaged in preaching. He had just come up from Salem when he was arrested and placed in jail. It is not clear what was the particular charge against him, if, indeed, there was any other than that of being a Quaker and in Boston, contrary to the ordinances which excluded these people. He was released, however, with numerous others, including his dear friend William Leddra, without undergoing any other suffering or indignity, and was ordered to leave the jurisdiction of Massachusetts, under penalty of death, if he should return.

The succession, in time and place, of the several persecutions of Friends in New-England, and of Wenlock Christison in particular, with whose sufferings we are now interested, it is exceedingly difficult to trace, for the martyrologist, Bishope, on whom we are compelled to rely in great measure, is singularly oblivious of dates and localities, and he frequently repeats the same dreadful story with variations in different connections, delighting in his theme. But it is pretty clear that after the banishment of Christison from Boston, he and his friends repaired to Plymouth, which, though one of the United Colonies, was not then within the jurisdiction of Massachusetts, nor was it until 1692. Here, however, Christison found the same laws prevailing and the same kind of magistrates ruling as were in the settlement from which he had been driven. He, accordingly, met with the same treatment, though with aggravated suffering. While Boston imprisoned and banished him, Plymouth subjected him not only to these punishments, but also to robbery, starvation, and to the pains and humiliations of personal chastisement. The account given of this sad affair as related by Bishope is here copied verbatim with all the quaint phraseology, with all the intense emphasis as expressed in capital letters, and with all the confusing disregard of punctuation, which belong to the original, and which characterizes the book. This book, it will be remembered, was addressed to the authorities and people of Boston. He says: "Where ['in Plimouth Patent'] Wenlock "Christison had been Imprisoned and Suffered "Twenty Seven cruel Stripes, on his naked Body, "at one time, laid on with Deliberation (so was "the Order of the Magistrates, who stood to see "it) in the cold Winter season, who bid the "Jaylor lay it on, who did it as hard as he could, "and then robbed him of his Wastcoat, (though

"in that cold time of the Year he was to pass
"through the Wilderness) and his Bible the Jay-
"lor took for Fees, who came about Midnight,
"much in drink, (so depriving him of the Scrip-
"tures) and then turning him out in the Morn-
"ing, having no Cloathes sufficient left to keep
"him Warm, Keeping him without Food, from
"the time of his cruel Whipping, to his turning
"out (he was five Days upon his first Commit-
"ment not suffered to have Food for his Money,)
"the Jaylor stopping up the Holes, saying, 'That
"at such places he might be supplied with Pro-
"visions;' keeping it so, until he asked them,
"'Whether they meant to Starve him,' after which
"they allowed him Provisions of three Pence a
"day, for five Weeks such as the Jaylor would
"give him; blood-thirsty Barloe [marshal of the
"three towns of Sandwich, Plymouth, and Yar-
"mouth] having also robbed him of his two other
"coats, and that and a Bag of Linnen, with up-
"wards of Four pounds, when he Apprehended
"him at Sandwich, after ye [the authorities of
"Boston] had Banished him on pain of Death,
"and kept him Fourteen Weeks and two Days
"in Prison, in the coldest time of the Winter.
"And thus he was Whipped, Robb'd and turned
"out, after Tho. Prince, the Governour and Magis-
"trates had caused him to be tied, Neck and
"Heels, for speaking for himself in Court, who

"denied him Satisfaction for his Goods, robb'd by
"Barloe, as aforesaid, when he was had at the
"Whipping-Post; with much a-do, he obtained
"so much Moderation of the Governour, as to
"hear him, who said in Answer,—'That he must
"first pay for his Preaching,' * * * and all this
"was but for coming into their Jurisdiction, when
"he was Banish'd out of yours."[1]

It would appear, therefore, that Wenlock Christison and his friend William Leddra, with other Friends, obeying the order of the court of Massachusetts, left the jurisdiction of that colony only to experience more cruel treatment in the older and adjoining settlement of Plymouth. But the penalty of death, which was to be inflicted upon them in case of their return to Boston, had no terrors with men for whom a death on the scaffold seemed to possess a fascination that lured them to attempt its accomplishment, and who coveted the glory of dying in the cause of "Truth and Light." Accordingly, we find that the orders of the magistrates were held as nothing when compared with the commands that were laid upon them, as they were fully persuaded, by a supreme authority. It is therefore not astonishing, when they felt the Spirit moving them to testify in those places from which they had been driven, that regardless of life, they again appeared in

[1] *New England Judged*, Part I, pp. 221-223.

Boston. This was not done in bravado, as some said, but in conformity with a sense of duty which was deemed imperative: although there is abundant evidence to show that however much the Friends may have disdained worldly distinctions, and those ornaments with which vanity seeks to adorn itself, they were nevertheless very emulous of saintly canonization, and felt a longing for that spiritual bauble, the crown of martyrdom. Governor Endicott, the court and the clergy especially, interpreted the conduct of these men differently, and as proceeding from a determination to brave and defy their power and authority. Accordingly, in the latter part of 1660, O. S., or in the early part of 1661, according to the new style, William Leddra, going to the jail in Boston to visit some Friends there imprisoned, was himself arrested, placed in irons, chained to a log, and suffered to lie in prison without fire, during a severe New England winter. On the 9th day of March, 1661, he was arraigned, in company with others, and refusing to accept his life on the condition of his leaving the Province and going back to England, he was put upon his trial, when there was no denial of the offences laid to his charge. While this trial was in progress, the proceedings had a most extraordinary interruption, which shall be related in the characteristic words of Bishope himself. * * * "But Wenlock

"Christison, being moved by the Lord, and
"brought by the Mighty Power of God, with
"his Life in his hand; and being made willing
"by the same Power & Life, to offer up his Life
"in Obedience to the Lord (in performance of
"which he found Peace & Rest) if he saw it
"good to require it of him, was not afraid of
"your Laws nor Gibbets, but in the Name and
"Power of God, tho' he stood in the Predicament
"of Death, having been already Banished by you,
"upon the 'Pain of Death,' came into your Court,
"not fearing the Wrath of the Devil, nor the
"Fury of the Dragon in you, which had Power
"to kill some, and persecute others of the Saints
"of the Most High God, even in the very time
"that you were trying the said W. Leddra, and
"there nobly shewed himself over the Head of
"all your Blood and Cruelty, in the strength of
"the Lord.

"This struck a great damp upon you, to see a
"Man so unconcern'd in his Life, to come upon
"your Law of Death, and trample it under, inso-
"much that for a little space of time there was
"Silence in the Court; but you recovering your
"Swoon, or the Spirit of Iniquity rising up over
"all in you again, you began to gather Strength,
"and recover Heart in your Wickedness, and
"one cries out, 'Here is another: Fetch him
"up to the Bar,' said you, which your Marshal

"performed, and bad him 'pluck of his Hat;'
"who said, 'No, I shall not.' Then said your
"Secretary, Rawson, 'Is not your name Wenlock
"Christison?' Wenlock said 'Yea.' Then said the
"Governour, John Endicot, unto him, after he
"had acknowledged his Name, (which he denied
"not, though in the face of Death) 'Wast thou
"not Banished upon Pain of Death?' Wenlock
"said, 'Yea, I was.' (See how Truth enables a
"Man to bear his Testimony, though the conse-
"quence be Death.) 'What dost thou here then?'
"said your Governour. He cried, 'That he was
"come to warn them that they should shed no
"more Innocent Blood; for the Blood that you
"have shed already, Cries unto the Lord God
"for Vengeance to come upon you.' Whereupon
"you said, 'Take him away Jaylor.'"[1] And to
jail he was sent, while his friend William Leddra
remained, to be tried and sentenced to death.
Three persons had already been hung for being
Quakers and for returning to the jurisdiction of
Massachusetts, after having been banished. These
were William Robinson, Marmaduke Stevenson,
and Mary Dyer, the two first named dying on
the 27th of October, 1759, and the one last mentioned on the 1st of April, 1660. William Leddra was sentenced on the 11th of March, and
was executed on the 14th of the same month,

[1] *New England Judged*, Part II., pp. 319-320.

1661, making the fourth and last victim of this cruel and senseless persecution that suffered death.

After the execution, and upon the very day that William Leddra was hung, the magistrates thinking "that his death would cool and bring under Wenlock Christison," and wishing, as is very clear, to save the life of this man, as well as vindicate their laws, had him arraigned before them. It was then said to him: "Unless you will renounce your religion you shall surely die." To this he firmly replied: "Nay, I shall not "change my religion, nor seek to save my life. "Neither do I intend to deny my Master. But "if I lose my Life for Christ's sake, and the "Preaching of the Gospel, I shall save it." The Court was amazed and confounded by this "Noble Valour for Truth." A friend, the same who subsequently prepared his grave cloathes, standing by, said: "Wenlock, Oh, thy turn is next." To whom Wenlock replied with fervor: "The will of the Lord be done." He was then remanded to prison to await the next term of the court to be held on the 3d of the fourth month, 1661. Before the time for the reassembling of the Court, there was apparently a reaction in the minds of the people and of the magistrates, with the exception of Governor Endicott. Consequently some hesitancy was shown, when the case was called, to proceed to the trial of Wenlock Christison;

and the Governor became enraged at this reluctance to enforce the laws—laws which he seemed not to perceive were not only ineffectual in arresting, but were most efficient in spreading the obnoxious doctrines and practices of these schismatics, the Quakers—for conversions were made under the very gallows, as in the case of John Chamberlaine, who was made a Quaker when William Leddra was hung. The Governor, after absenting himself, in his anger, for two days from the court, was prevailed upon to return, the magistrates having consented to proceed with the trial of Christison. It was a prevalent sentiment of that day, in which Friends as religious enthusiasts were participant, and one that is not entirely dispelled at the present, that nature sometimes manifests a sympathy with man in his joys or sorrows, by an inversion of her laws, and by giving birth to "signs and wonders." It is not strange that the mind of the writer of the book, from which all these circumstances have been gathered, should have been prone to see a connection between some unusual natural phenomena and the painful events he was relating. Accordingly, we find him stating that for two weeks, during which the "conspiracies of blood" were revolving in the minds of the judges and others engaged in the prosecution, "the natural "Sun in the firmament shone not"—"a remarka-

"ble demonstration of the displeasure of the
"Lord, and a true figure and representation of
"this your wickness and work."

At last Wenlock Christison was brought to the bar for his trial, of which Bishope in his book has given this most singular account: "So you
"being agreed, before the Judgment Seat Wen-
"lock was brought; who thither came in a good
"Dominion, because he felt the Power of God
"over all; who being there set, your Governour
"asked him, 'What he had to say for himself;
"why he might not Dye?' 'I have done nothing
"worthy of Death,' (replied Wenlock) 'if I had,
"I refuse not to Dye.' 'Thou art come in amongst
"us' (said another of you) 'in Rebellion, which
"is as the Sin of Witchcraft, and ought to be
"punished.' 'I came not in among you in Re-
"bellion' (answered Wenlock), 'but in Obedience
"to the God of Heaven; not in Contempt to any
"of you, but in Love to your Souls and Bodies;
"and that you shall know one day, when you
"and all men must give an Account of your
"Deeds done in the Body. 'Take heed' (said he)
"'for you cannot escape the Righteous Judg-
"ments of God.' Then said your Major-General,
"Adderton, 'You pronounce Woes and Judg-
"ments, and those that are gone before you pro-
"nounced Woes and Judgments; but the Judg-
"ments of the Lord God are not come upon us

"yet.' 'Be not Proud' (reply'd Wenlock) 'neither
"let your Spirits be lifted up; God doth but
"wait, till the measure of your Iniquity be filled
"up, and that you have run your ungodly Race,
"then will the Wrath of God come upon you
"to the uttermost: And as for thy part, it hangs
"over thy head, and is near to being poured
"down upon thee; and shall come as a Thief
"in the Night suddenly, when thou thinkest not
"of it.' 'By what Law' (said Wenlock) 'will ye
"put me to Death?' 'We have a law' (reply'd
"you) 'and by our Law you are to Dye.' 'So
"said the Jews of Christ' (Wenlock reply'd). 'We
"have a Law, and by our Law he ought to Dye.'
"'Who empowered you to make that Law,' (said
"he)? One of you answered, 'We have a Patent,
"and are the Patentees, judge whether we have
"not the power to make laws.' Wenlock reply'd
"again, 'How, have you power to make laws re-
"pugnant to the Laws of England?' 'Nay,'
"said your Governour. 'Then' (answered Wen-
"lock) 'you are gone beyond your Bounds, and
"have forfeited your Patent; and this is more
"than you can answer.' And he cryed out, and
"said, 'Are you Subjects to the King, yea or
"nay?' 'What good will that do you,' replyed
"your Secretary? 'What will you infer from
"that?' Wenlock answered, 'If you are, say so,
"for in your Petition to the King, you desire

"that he would protect you, and that you may
"be worthy to Kneel amongst his Royal Subjects;
"or words to that effect.' To which one of you
"said, 'Yea.' Then Wenlock answered and said,
"'So am I; and for any thing I know, am as
"good as you, if not better; for if the King did
"but know your Hearts, as God knows them, he
"would see that your Hearts are as rotten towards
"him, as they are towards God. Therefore seeing
"that you and I are Subjects to the King, I
"demand to be tried by the Laws of my own
"Nation.' 'You shall be tried' (reply'd you) 'by
"a Bench and a Jury.' 'That is not the Law'
"(said Wenlock) 'but the manner of it; for if
"you will be as good as your word, you must
"set me at Liberty; for I never heard or read,
"of any Law that was in England to Hang Qua-
"kers.' Your Governour reply'd, 'That there was
"a Law to Hang Jesuits.' Wenlock answered,
"'If you put me to Death it is not because I go
"under the Name of a Jesuit, but a Quaker;
"therefore' (said he) 'I do Appeal to the Laws
"of my own Nation.' Then one of you said,
"'That he was in your Hands, and had broken
"your Law, and you would try him.' Wenlock
"deny'd to be tried by your Law; yet the Jury
"you caused to be called over, and you told him
"'He had liberty to object against them, or any
"of them.' Wenlock still appealed to the Law

"of his own Nation; but still you cried out,
"'That you would try him;' and so deny'd his
"Appeal. 'Then' (said Wenlock) 'your Will is
"your Law, and what you have power to do, that
"you will do: And seeing that the Jury must
"go forth on my Life, this I have to say to you,
"in the Fear of the Living God, Jury, take heed
"what you do, for you Swear by the living God,
"That you will true trial make, and just Verdict
"give, according to the Evidence: Jury, look for
"your Evidence, what have I done worthy of
"Death? Keep your hands out of innocent
"Blood.' To which one of the Jury reply'd, 'It
"is good Counsel.' So away they went, but hav-
"ing received their lesson from you, and being
"of the same Spirit, quickly brought him in
"Guilty; whereupon your Secretary said, 'Wen-
"lock Christison hold up your Hand.' 'I will
"not' (said Wenlock), 'for my Conscience is clear
"in the sight of God.' Your Governour an-
"swered, 'The Jury hath condemned thee.' But
"he answered, 'The Lord doth justifie me, who
"art thou that condemnest?'"

After the rendition of the verdict by the jury, there arose a diversity of opinion among the members of the court, whether the sentence of death, or some milder punishment, should be inflicted upon Wenlock Christison. The Governour, Endicott, who is represented as *thirsting* for the blood of the innocent, flew into a violent rage that there should be any hesitancy to inflict the extreme penalty of the law. This rage was aggravated by the reception, at this very moment, of a letter from one *Edward Wharton*, who had previously been condemned and ordered into banishment, under penalty of death should he return, stating coolly that he was at home, in his own house, had not gone into banishment, did not mean to go, and then demanding to be released from his sentence that he might go about his "occasions." This defiant letter caused the Governor to break out into a furious passion. He threw the thing he had in his hand, whatever it may have been, possibly some emblem of office, violently upon the table, as he sat in the judgment seat, and exclaimed: "I could find it in my heart to go "Home." Wenlock replied: "It were better for "thee to be at home, than here, for thou art "about a bloody piece of work." The vote of the court was then taken, but some still refused to sanction the death of the prisoner at the bar. The Governor, in a greater rage than ever, "stood "up and said: 'You that will not consent, Record "it,' and like a man drunk, he said, 'Thank God, "I am not afraid to give judgment. Wenlock "Christison, hearken to your Sentence. You must "return unto the place from whence you came, "and from thence to the place of Execution, and

"there you must be hanged until you be dead,
"dead, dead, upon the thirteenth day of June,
"being the fifth Day of the Week.' Which being
"thus cruelly pronounced, Wenlock Christison
"called out, and said 'The Will of the Lord be
"done in whose Will I came amongst you, and
"in his Counsel I stand, feeling his eternal Power,
"that will uphold me until the last Gasp, I do
"not Question it.' Moreover, he cried, saying,
"'Known be it unto you all, That if you have
"power to take my life from me, that my Soul
"shall enter into everlasting Rest and Peace
"with God, where you yourselves shall never
"come: And if you have power to take my life
"from me, the which I do question, I do believe
"you shall never more take Quakers' lives from
"them (note my words) do not think to weary
"out the living God by taking away the Lives
"of his Servants! What do you gain by it?
"For the last Man that you put to Death here
"are five come in his Room: And if you have
"power to take my Life from me, God can raise
"up the same Principle of Life in Ten of his
"Servants, and send them among you, in my
"room, that you may have Torment upon Tor-
"ment, which is your Portion; For there is no
"Peace to the Wicked saith my God.' Then the
"Governor said 'take him away' and to prison
"he was sent."[1]

[1] *New England Judged*, Part II., pp. 336-340

Unquestionably, while these severe proceedings against the Quakers were in progress, a reaction was taking place in the popular mind in Massachusetts and all the New England settlements—a reaction, if not favorable to actual toleration, at least to a more lenient treatment of the obnoxious schismatics, and rebels against authority. It was revolting to men whose fathers, or they themselves, had left their native country that they might enjoy a freedom of worship, that a harmless fanaticism, for such they esteemed Quakerism to be, should be treated with such severity as to lead some to the gibbet. It began to be discovered that the excesses, foolish or wicked, into which some of this body had fallen, were not countenanced by the Friends, and therefore punishment for these should not be visited upon those who were innocent of them. In the minds of the authorities, too, this same reaction in favor of milder measures was taking place, but with them there was another efficient cause for the adoption of more lenient treatment of offenders. This was the apprehension that the King did not approve of their extreme conduct towards the Friends. The first part of Bishope's book, from which quotation has been so liberally made, had been circulated in England, and had served, with similar publications, to awaken public attention to the enormities practised in America upon the

Quakers. The King himself had been listening to the representations of persons friendly to these persecuted people; and corrupt and vile as he was, he was neither cruel nor fanatical. A man of the easy self-indulgent habits of Charles II, was not willing to allow his pleasures to be disturbed or marred, nor his equanimity to be shaken by the cries of certain of his subjects, or by the indulgence of the malign passions of certain others. He was therefore persuaded to issue a royal mandate to Governor Endicott, and all other Governors of New England, granting full and free toleration to all sects for the exercise of their religion and exempting Quakers from the punishment of death for any other offences than those for which that penalty was adjudged by the laws of England. The order was no sooner signed than it was given into the charge of a special messenger to be conveyed to those to whom it was addressed. Sam'l Shattuck, who was one of those had been banished from Massachusetts, and who were under penalty of death in case of their return to that jurisdiction, was the messenger selected, and he took passage in a ship chartered for the purpose by Friends in England. Before the arrival of Shattuck, however, at least before the delivery of the royal letter, the authorities at Boston had received intimation of what had been accomplished with the King, and determined to make a merit of doing that, before the command was received, which the command itself would require should be done. An ordinance or new law was passed, abolishing so much of the old law as permitted the infliction of capital punishment upon Quakers. So on Tuesday following the pronouncing the sentence upon Wenlock Christison, which was on Thursday, but the precise date is not recorded, the Marshal and a Constable came to the prison, where he, with twenty-seven other prisoners, "Friends of Truth," lay confined for their "Testimony to the Truth;" but "resting in sweet Peace and Quietness of Spirit," bearing an order from the court for their "enlargement." The Marshal said to Wenlock and his companions, "'They were ordered by the Court to make them "acquainted with their new Law.' Then said "Wenlock, 'What means this? Have you a new "Law?' 'Yes,' said they. 'Then you have de-"ceived most people,' said Wenlock. 'Why?' "said they. 'Because,' said Wenlock, 'they did "think the gallows had been your last weapon; "Have you got more yet?' 'Yes,' said they. "'Read it,' said Wenlock, which they did. He "began to taunt the officers with the vacillation "and timidity of the magistrates. Then Wenlock "said, 'Your Magistrates said that your law was a "good and wholesome Law, made for your Peace "and the safeguard of your country: What are "your Hands, now become weak? The Power of "God is over all?'" Here Bishope breaks forth into the following canticle of exultation: "Then "the Prison Doors were set open, and Twenty "seven more, beside Wenlock were turned forth, "as aforesaid, whereof two [Peter Pearson and "Judith Brown] were stripp'd to the Waste, and "made fast to a Cart's Tail, and whipped through "the Town of Boston with twenty cruel stripes "on their naked Backs and Shoulders; Many "mouths were opened, and the mighty Day of "the dreadful God was sounded forth by the "Servants of the Mighty God, who wrought De-"liverance for his chosen vessels: So, into the "Wilderness they were driven by your Sword "and Club-men, who had received order from "you thus to force them out of your Jurisdiction; "which they performed: Glory, Glory be given "unto the Lord over all, saith my Soul, who "never leaves nor forsakes the Righteous, but "redeems his faithful Ones out of all their Trou-"bles: Praise the Lord all his Saints, who are "upon the Rock of Ages: and the Gates of "Hell cannot prevail against you, saith Wenlock "Christison."[1]

[1] *New England Judged*, Part II., pp. 340-341.

PALFREY, in his *History of New England*, (vol. II., p. 481,) gives a slightly different account of the release of the prisoners, to wit: they were not released until the mandamus of the King had been received by

Thus terminated this remarkable trial. It has been given in all its details as far as they can be gleaned from the book of George Bishope, not only because the incidents are extremely interesting in themselves and illustrative of the man around whom they cluster, as well as of the class of people with whom he was allied by religious sympathy; but because they are profoundly suggestive to the reflecting mind of inferences bearing upon the philosophy of human character and conduct.

For the space of about two years the Friends in New England and all the colonies enjoyed peace and quiet under the royal mandate; for when this had been received and read it was found to be very thorough and comprehensive, not only forbidding the taking of the lives of Quakers, or other sectaries, but forbidding the infliction of any punishment whatever, on account of their religion. Toleration so complete, neither

the Governor, who said with the promptness and subservience of a courtier, "We shall obey his Majesty's command."

PALFREY also gives a paper, found among the archives of the State of Massachusetts, signed by Wenlock Christison, which indicates that his fortitude had given way before his release, and that he was ready to regain his freedom by leaving the colony. The following is a copy of this paper:

"I, the condemned man, doe give forth under my Hand, that, if I may "have my liberty, I have freedome to depart this Jurisdiction; and I "know not y't ever I shall com into it any more.

"WINLOCK CHRISTISON.

" From y'e gaol in Boston,
"Ye 7th day of ye 4th mo. 1661,"

the people nor the authorities were prepared to accept. So interest was made at Court to have the royal command so far modified as to permit so-called mild punishments to be visited upon those who made themselves offensive by their principles or practices; and the easy King yielded to the importunities of his faithful subjects in New England, who were becoming profuse in their expressions of loyalty, whatever may have been their secret feelings. Accordingly, we find the persecutions were renewed, and Quakers were arrested, imprisoned, fined, whipped and banished as before, but no one suffered death after the hanging of William Leddra. One Edward Wharton, whose letter to Governor Endicott. demanding his unconditional release and pardon, caused that dignitary to loose his equilibrium in open court, was a particularly obnoxious subject to the magistrates. He was often punished, but apparently without the slightest effect upon his conduct. John Chamberlaine, who was convinced under the very gallows, at the execution of Will Leddra, was another sufferer. He was beaten no less than nine times, and as many banished. He seemed to be in love with the lash. But to mention all those who were punished, would be both tedious and useless. The worst cases, however, were those of women, even old and weakly women, who were imprisoned, banished, stripped, whipped at the cart's tail through the towns, thrown headlong down stairs, accused of witchcraft and half drowned in the rivers. The cruelties and outrages that were inflicted upon them are so atrocious that credulity is taxed to the utmost to credit the accounts which Bishope gives of them in his book of horrors.

After the release of Wenlock Christison and his fellow-sufferers from the Boston jail, in 1661, and his expulsion from the jurisdiction of Massachusetts, little information can be obtained of him for several years. He is mentioned more than once incidentally by Bishope, apparently during the time from 1661 to 1664; but this writer is so confused in his chronology, that it is quite impossible to determine the dates of many of the events he narrates. Christison appears to have traveled about from place to place, among Friends. At one time he was in Rhode Island, at another at Salem, at another at Hampton, in what is now New Hampshire. At this last named town we hear of him in connection with one Eliakim Wardel, a resident of that place, and a Friend. It appears that Eliakim Wardel, contrary to the law, gave him entertainment or hospitality, and was fined therefor; but refusing to pay the fine, his horse was seized, "a pretty beast for the saddle, worth about fourteen pound." This same Eliakim was again arrested at the instigation of one Seaborn Cotton, a clergyman, for a like offence in receiving W. Christison "in the name of a Disciple." On this occasion Christison showed that, serious a man as he was and full of sorrows, he was not without a kind of grim humor, and was not at all intimidated by the fierce laws against Quakers, nor by the executors of those laws. Indeed he had shown something of the same kind of humor upon other occasions. Seaborn Cotton, "the Priest," came to arrest Eliakim, accompanied by the constables and posse; or, in the words of Bishope, "like a Sturdy "Herdsman, he got to him some of the fiercest "of his swine, and himself at the head of them, "with a Leader's Truncheon in his hand." Wenlock Christison meeting these people as they approached Eliakim's house, asked Cotton, "What he did with that Club in his hand." Cotton answered, "He came to keep the Wolves from his Sheep." Wenlock, pointing to the rough fellows that accompanied Cotton, asked derisively, "Whether these were his sheep," and impliedly asked if Eliakim and he were the wolves to be kept off. This enraged Cotton, but the keen satire did not deter him from ordering his lambs to carry off the Quaker wolves. The dates of these incidents are not known; but on the 30th. June, 1664, we find Christison again in Boston, whither he had come from Salem to meet Mary Tomkins and Alice Gary, two female apostles, who had just returned from Virginia, where they had not escaped a persecution similar to that they had endured in New England; for there, too, they had suffered the pain and indignity of being whipped, receiving "thirty-two stripes apiece, with "a nine corded whip, three knots in each cord, "being drawn up to a pillory in such an uncivil "manner as is not to be rehearsed, with a run-"ning knot above the hands, the very first lash "of which drew Blood, and made it run down " in abundance from their Breasts," and had been robbed of their goods for fines imposed upon them, and finally "expelled those Coasts."[1] To see these returning friends, Wenlock Christison and Edward Wharton came from Salem, and they, with the women, were arrested, convicted of being within the jurisdiction from which they had been banished, and were sentenced, as usual, to be whipped through the towns. But a Col. Temple and the wife of the Governor interceded in their behalf, and all were exempt from this suffering except Edward Wharton, who was condemned to be bound to the wheel of "a great

---

[1] *New England Judged*, Part II, p. 440   This persecution of Mary Tomkins and Alice Gary in Virginia is here mentioned for the purpose of proving what was before asserted, that the Quakers received the same treatment, except in the four cases of hanging, among the ancestors of those who most reproach the New Englanders, as they received among the people of Massachusetts.

gun," and to receive thirty stripes, which was executed in such a cruel manner, says Bishope, "That Pease might lie in the Holes that the "Knots of the Whip had beat into the Flesh of "his arms and back."

In the early part of the year 1665, as near as can be determined, Wenlock Christison was again apprehended for being in Boston, contrary to law, and carried before deputy Governor Bellingham, Endicott being just now dead, when this colloquy took place between the prisoner at the bar and the court: "Your Deputy, Bel-"lingham, said, 'He should be whipp'd.' Wen-"lock demanded, 'For what?' Your Deputy said, "'Because he was a Vagabond.' 'Then,' replied "Wenlock, 'Cain was a Vagabond, he slew his "Brother, yet he was great in the Earth and "built a city. And' said Wenlock, 'What is a "Vagabond as saith your Law?' One of Cain's "stock answered, 'Such as have no certain dwell-"ing place.' 'How do you know,' (said Wen-"lock) 'that I have no certain dwelling place?' "It was answered, 'You have none amongst us.' "'Are all Vagabonds,' reply'd Wenlock, 'that "have no dwelling place among you? If it be "so, then go and Whip out the King's Commis-"sioners[1] from among you for they came out of

[1] These Commissioners were Nicols, Carr and Cartwright, who came out from England in 1664, to whom was added Maverick, of Massachusetts. They were authorized to examine into certain complaints that had been laid before the King of wrongs and encroachments upon the neigh-

"England since I did; they do hire Rooms, and
"carry the Keys in their Pockets, and so can I.'
"And he said, 'I have money in my Pocket and
"Cloaths to wear, and a Beast to ride on, And
"what is a Vagabond, saith your Law? At this
"Bar' (said he) 'time was, the Sentence of Death
"was passed on me, yet, by the help of God, I
"continue unto this Day, standing over the Heads
"of you all, bearing a faithful Witness for the
"Truth of the living God: Some of your Asso-
"ciates are gone, and the Lord hath laid their
"Glory in the Dust, and yours is a fading
Flower.'" The prisoner was then ordered to be
carried to jail. Wenlock when arraigned the next
day appealed to the Laws of England, and accused
the court of violating the King's order of 1661,
guaranteeing Liberty of Conscience. He then appealed to the King's Commissioners. The Court
replied, "'We are Commissioners, and more
"than Commissioners.' Then Wenlock said, 'Do
"you own these men whom the King has sent
"among you?' Some one replyed, 'We will let
"that alone now.' And another said, 'If thou
"hadst been Hanged, it had been well.' 'You
"had Power,' reply'd Wenlock, 'to take away my

boring settlements and upon the Indians: also to settle certain controversies respecting boundaries. The appointment of this Commission was the occasion of some solicitude in Massachusetts, as boding ill to its charter. The members were not, therefore, received with that cordiality that personages so conspicuous and bearing a royal commission had a right to expect.

"life from me; but my Blood is upon you, for
"you murthered me in your Hearts.' So Wen-
"lock, Mary Tomkins and Alice Ambrose, [or
"Gary], were stripped to the Waste, and made
"fast to the Cart and whipp'd through Boston,
"Roxbury and Denham. Wenlock had ten cruel
"Stripes, in each Town, and the other two, his
"Companions, six apiece. They were driven
"into the wilderness, but the Lord was with them
"& the Angel of his Presence saved them, who
"had none in Heaven besides God, and none on
"Earth in Comparison of Him. Let the Living
"sing Glory to the Highest, saith Wenlock Chris-
"tison."[1]

In this account of the examination or trial of
Christison there are two points worthy of notice:
his own ingenuity, and the ascription to him of
prophetic powers. It was a very usual expedient
of the Quakers, when arraigned before the court, to
try to turn the tables on the judges, by entrap-
ping them into some expression which should
show the disaffection they actually felt to the
royal government, and thus to discredit them with
the King, whose favor they were at the same
time solicitous of retaining: or by affecting to
catch them in some profane, irreverent or hereti-
cal words which, in a theocracy such as then
existed in Massachusetts, might be so interpreted

[1] *New England Judged*, Part II., pp. 458-159.

as to bring them into disrepute or contempt with those people who gave tone to public opinion. In this case Christison hoped to involve the court in a conflict with the royal commissioners, whose presence at that time in Massachusetts was a matter of much serious though secret discontent with the authorities, as threatening the modification or abrogation of their chartered privileges. We have here another instance of Quaker simplicity and plainness disguising the highest tact and most delicate finesse. The other point to be noticed is, that Christison's reference to the death of Endicott, and the fading of the flower of the court, that is, to the decline of its power, was regarded by Bishope as predicting evil to the judges, or as prophetic in its character; although it is difficult to perceive upon what grounds he based his opinions. This was not the only occasion when the words of Christison, uttered under great exaltation of feeling, were thought to be vaticinal, and accounts are given of the actual accomplishment of many of his alleged predictions—notably, of the sudden death, by a fall from his horse, of Major General Adderton. It does not appear that he himself consciously claimed prophetic powers, but evidently he regarded his words as prompted by a divine intelligence, and his prognostications of evil to come upon his persecutors and their country as something more than the anticipations of human reason or the denunciations of human passion.

It would appear that Christison and his companions in suffering, after being driven from Massachusetts, took refuge in Rhode Island, where there was an asylum always open for those who would escape religious intolerance, under Roger Williams, himself a banished and persecuted man, or his successors in the Presidency of that colony.[1] But either impelled by a desire to preach the "Truth" in foreign parts, or at last wearied out with the cruel persecutions of New England, all three of those mentioned came up to Boston from the Providence plantations under the protection of one of the King's commissioners, Sir Robert Carr,[2] for the purpose of taking ship, Wenlock Christison for Barbadoes, and the two women for the Bermudas. Here they met other Friends from Salem — the inevitable and irrepressible Edward Wharton, of course, being of the num-

[1] Roger Williams offered an asylum to the Friends, to be sure, and while within his jurisdiction they were free from persecution, or any personal violence; but though he proved himself a friend of Quakers, he was an enemy of Quakerism, as he showed in the celebrated controversy which he held with three of their ministers in 1672, at New-port, and in his book, written against them, entitled "George Fox Digged out of his Burrows." Here was true toleration! to bear with that which he condemned.

[2] This Sir Robt. Carr was he who reduced the Dutch forts upon the Delaware, driving out the brave Governor Alexander De Hinniossa, or d'Hinojossa, or as he calls himself, d'Hinoyossa, who took refuge in Maryland, and settled in Talbot county. An original memoir of this worthy has been published by the author of this paper, as a part of the biographical history of Talbot.

ber; for whenever kindness was to be shown to Friends, or suffering to be endured by them—why may it not be said, suffering enjoyed? for verily these good people went to it and seemed to seek after it as though it were the delight of their life to suffer for the cause of "Truth"—there Edward Wharton was certain to be present. This was in May, 1665. The constables were soon on the alert to ferret out the "Cursed Quakers as you call them whom the Lord calls Blessed," as Bishope says. They were not hard to find, and were soon arraigned before Deputy Governor Bellingham. As preparatory to the serious work of the trial or examination, Bellingham said his prayers, and the "irreverent gestures" of the prisoners, and their "sitting and walking about with their hats upon their heads" during his devotions were made one of the grounds of action against them. The trial was soon dispatched and Wenlock Christison, Edward Wharton and Alice Gary[1] were sentenced to be whipped through three towns, out of the jurisdiction, but Wharton being an old and hardened offender, was imprisoned as well as beaten.

After this trial, for standing with his hat upon his head during the Governor's devotions, Bishope

---

[1] This Alice Ambrose, alias Gary, there is good reason to believe, settled at West-River in Maryland. She is one of those mentioned in the will of Peter Sharpe, hereafter to be noticed.

in his book makes no further mention of Wenlock Christison, and we have no account of his movements for some years. We lose sight of him as he is driven forth with blows into the wilderness, a wanderer, without certain home, truly a vagabond, but not in an opprobrious sense, imprisoned, starved, robbed, beaten, outlawed. When we catch glimpses of him again, it is under more auspicious circumstances. We find him settled in his own quiet home, sitting at his own fireside, in the midst of loving wife and children. We find him surrounded by honoring friends and neighbors, occupying the seat of the elders among the Friends, without fear of pillory, jail, or constable's whip. We find him protected by benign laws, and even daring to stand covered—precious privilege!—in the presence of Governors and magistrates. We find him, in short, in tolerant Maryland and in beautiful Talbot.

From the known character of Friends, whom no amount of suffering deterred from following a course which they verily believed was marked out for them by a divine hand, it is not likely that Wenlock Christison, and his two women friends, were diverted from their purpose to visit the societies which had been formed in the Bermudas and the Barbadoes; but it is altogether probable that very soon after their last trial and punishment by Governor Bellingham, in May, 1665, they carried their design into successful execution, and that they escaped out of the "bloody town of Boston," as Bishope calls it, and the "Habitations of Cruelty" of New England. The journey to the West Indies was only a part of that wide circuit of travel which was followed by many of the early Quaker preachers, which circuit was completed by going from those islands to Virginia and Maryland, and thence "through the woods" to Long Island, where there was a society at Oyster-Bay, and back again to New England. At the period of these events Pennsylvania had not been founded by Penn, nor the settlements of Quakers in Jersey under Fenwick and Billings established. Religion, when not the pioneer, is always the follower of commerce, keeping to its track. At the time of these events, there was an active intercourse between the West India Islands and the New England colonies, and also between those islands and the settlements of Virginia and Maryland. But conjecture aside, it is known from actual and authoritative records that Wenlock Christison, and one, at least, of those women with whom he last suffered in Boston, were in Maryland as early as 1670, and perhaps before. There is no doubt whatever, that he himself was living in Talbot county as early as 1670. Thus:

In the Register's office of Calvert county there is recorded the will of Peter Sharpe, "chirurgion," who is also called "Peter Sharpe of the Cliffs,"[1] meaning the clifts of the Patuxent, (in Liber No. 1, for years 1635 to 1674,) bearing the date of the year 1672. The following is an extract from this will:[2]

"I give to Friends in ye Ministry, viz: Alice "Gary, William Cole and Sarah Marsh, if then

[1] This Peter Sharpe is the same person from whom the island in the mouth of Great Choptank river takes the name it now very improperly bears. This island has been known by several names, according as it has belonged to this or that person, but the name of the Quaker physician of Calvert has clung to it, and will be ever used to designate a little patch of earth (originally 700 acres), diminishing year by year and destined, at no very remote geological period, to disappear beneath the waves of the Chesapeake, unless, indeed, there shall be another of those secular upheavals which first lifted it and the whole Eastern Shore out of the sea. But if priority of designation should be allowed to govern, the proper name of this island is *Claiborne*. In the deed of Will Sharpe, son and heir of Peter, to John Eason, (Sept. 10, 1675,) it is expressly stated that this island "was formerly known by the name of *Claiborn's Island*, and now or lately by the name of Sharpe's Island " This is repeated in other and subsequent conveyances. There is little doubt that Col. William Claiborne, the original settler, if he may not claim the honor of founder, of Maryland, visited, took possession of, and gave his name to this island. All the world knows, that before the "Maryland Pilgrims," so-called, came in he had established a trading post on Kent Point. under the Virginia charter, and it is believed his friend and follower, Richard Thompson, held, under him, Poplar Island also. Poplar Island has a distinction in the local annals of Talbot as having been long the residence of Alexander De Hinniossa, the last Dutch Governor of Delaware, after the seizure of that settlement by the English in the year 1664. It is really due to Claiborne, whom Lord Baltimore's colonists treated so badly, and who has fared so poorly at the hands of the historians, that his name should be permanently attached to some spot of earth in a State the seeds of whose civilization he was the first to plant. Historic justice and the laws of geographical nomenclature demand that this island, while any of it remains, shall be called Claiborne's Island.

[2] G. L. L. Davis's "Day Star," p. 78.

"in being; Wenlock Christison and his wife;
"John Burnett[1] and Daniel Gould;[2] in money
"or goods, at the choice of my executors, forty
"shillings worth apiece; also for a perpetual
"standing, a horse, for the use of Friends in ye
"ministry, and to be placed at the convenient
"place for their use."

But there is a yet earlier record of the presence of Wenlock Christison in Maryland, and of his being a resident of Talbot county—a record in which the name of Peter Sharpe is mentioned in connection with him. From the land records of this county (No. 1, Fol. 120), it appears that on the first of August, 1670, Peter Sharpe of the clifts of Calvert, surgeon, and Judith his wife, transferred to Wenlock Christison, "in con-
"sideration of true affection and brotherly love
"which we have and beare unto our well beloved
"brother Wenlock Christison, in Talbot county,
"and also for other divers good causes and con-
"siderations, wee at this present especially mov-
"ing," one hundred and fifty acres of land, part of Fausley, on Fausley creek, south side of Saint Michæl's river, and known by the name of "Ending of Controversie." What more appropriate name could there be for the home of a

---

[1] This is doubtless John Burneyeat, who traveled through this region before Fox and then with him.

[2] Daniel Gould was one of those who suffered in England as early as 1661. It is not certain that he settled in Maryland, though probable.

man whose life had been spent in strife and disputation! It will not escape notice that this conveyance expresses no other consideration but that of "true affection and brotherly love." There can be but little doubt that the good Quaker physician of Calvert, who was a man of large possessions, bestowed this little farm upon the poor wanderer because of his sympathy for him in his sufferings and privations, and in recognition of his services in the cause of "Truth and Light." This gift of land was not the only act of kindness on the part of Peter Sharpe towards Wenlock Christison. He, as has just been shown, with others, was remembered in the will of the Calvert worthy, and had a legacy of two pounds sterling—not an insignificant sum at a time when and in a place where money was so scarce and worth many times as much as now.

Nor was Peter Sharpe the only sympathizing friend who bestowed wordly goods on Christison. What was land worth unless it could be cultivated, and what could he do with one hundred and fifty acres of wild land, covered with heavy timber, and perhaps not one acre under the plough—he, a preacher, often called away on long journeys, having "a concern to visit Friends," as the phraseology of Quakers was, in distant quarters? Henry Wilcocks, another Friend, sets about remedying this trouble, and on the 31st. of March, 1671, he, for no consideration as far as expressed in the conveyance, assigns and makes over to him a servant man named Francis Lloyd. This was really a valuable addition to his wealth, for labor was then, as now, the great want and demand of the people of Talbot, and indentured servants were sought after with even greater avidity than the farmers of this county are now seeking German emigrants. Other records for 1675 and 1676 show that Christison became possessed of other servants, probably by purchase, for in the former year he brought his servant Edward Gibson into court to have his age and time of service adjudged, according to a custom then in vogue, and in the latter year he brought his servant John Stacy before the justices for a similar purpose. As evidence of the kindly relations which subsisted between these indentured servants, bought from the emigrant ships, and their masters, it may be mentioned that this John Stacy was set free by the will of Christison, who left to him legacies in consideration of his fidelity and good behavior. But Christison became the possessor not only of white servants, but, it will be seen in the sequel, he was interested in the ownership of colored ones also.

In 1673 he obtained from John Edmondson, another Friend, one hundred acres of land apparently adjoining that derived from Peter Sharpe. In 1677 he became the owner of another tract, in the same section of the county, which had been in the possession of one John Davis, and known by the name of "Ashby," of which Roger Gross was the original patentee. In neither of these cases is any consideration mentioned as having been given; so these properties, too, may have been acquired through the brotherly love and affection of the owners. Wenlock Christison, therefore, seems to have prospered, having become the possessor of broad estates and troops of servants, verifying the truth of the declaration of the great founder of doctrinal Christianity respecting the worldly profitableness of godliness.

From what is here said of the lands acquired by Christison, whether by gift or purchase, the place of his residence may be determined with almost absolute precision. There is no doubt that he owned and resided upon that point of land which is formed by what is now called "Glebe" and "Goldsborough's creeks," and now (1874) owned by Mr. Addison Randall—one of the most charming sites in Talbot county and adorned by the beautiful villa built by Mr. Richard France. It is certain he owned a part of the large tract of "Fausley," which received the name of "Ending of Controversie." Family tradition establishes the fact that the residence of William Dixon who married the widow and obtained the estate of Christison, and who bequeathed this estate, in the absence of direct heirs of his body, to his nephew Isaac Dixon, was the brick dwelling standing in a dilapidated condition upon the "Woodstock" property, which now embraces a part of "Fausley"[1] and a part of "End of Controversie." Before the erection of houses of worship throughout the county of Talbot, and indeed occasionally after the building of those houses, it was customary for Friends to hold their meetings at the private residences of some of the more conspicuous members of the Society, selecting those which were most central or most easily accessible. Those who are familiar with the topography of Talbot will perceive, from what has been said, that the house of Christison was so situated that

[1] "Fausley" has another title to celebrity besides that of having been once in the ownership of the Quaker worthy. Here were born two persons who occupy no inconspicuous place in their country's history, namely, Col. Tench Tilghman, Secretary and Aide to Gen'l Washington during the whole war of independence, and his brother, the Hon William Tilghman, the distinguished Chief Justice of the Supreme Court of Pennsylvania. Of the former Gen'l Washington said: "He left as fair a reputation as ever belonged to human character." A memoir of him has been published, written by the author of this paper. Of Chief Justice Tilghman Mr. Horace Binney said in an eulogy of unsurpassed eloquence, in the reading of which one is at a loss to determine which was more fortunate, Mr. Tilghman in having such an eulogist, or Mr. Binney in having such a subject for his eulogium: "It will be long, very long, "before we shall open our eyes upon a wiser judge, a sounder lawyer, a "riper scholar, a purer man or a truer gentleman."

it was very central, and that it could be conveniently approached from all parts of the county, either by land or water. In those early days, the beautiful rivers and creeks of that portion of the Eastern shore were more generally used for local travel and transportation than now, and the canoe and barge then took the place, in the absence of carriage roads, of the wheeled vehicles which are now so commonly employed. At that time nearly all the settlements were along the water courses, and inasmuch as the geographical formation of Talbot is such that almost every man's house may be upon navigable water, that county was very early completely taken up and settled. Christison's house could not have been more than a mile and a half or two miles, by water, from the meeting house of Friends first erected upon the Eastern Shore of the State, namely, that at Betty's Cove. This house was upon the land now owned by Mr. Robt. Dixon, who holds to the faith and observes the customs of those who originally erected this little sanctuary in the primitive wilderness. It was at this house that George Fox preached when he was in Talbot in 1672, when he saw, as he says in his journal, the river covered with boats almost as numerous as upon the Thames at London, and filled with people coming to hear him discourse.[1] In the house of Wenlock Christison, near Betty's Cove meeting house, the first meeting of Friends, of which there is any official record of proceedings, ever held in Maryland, took place. This was what was called a "Man's Meeting," or a meeting for business and not for worship. It assembled on the 4th of April, 1677, for the purpose of considering the matter of having the meeting house at Betty's Cove improved and repaired; for it would appear that this house had become too small to accommodate the growing society, and had been erected a sufficiently long time, at that date, to need repairs.[2]

His being the recipient of legacies and gifts of money, lands and servants, attests the affection with which Christison was regarded by

[1] The Friends generally believe that the meeting house in which George Fox preached when he was in Talbot in the year 1672, was the "Great Meeting House at Third Haven," yet standing near Easton and still used as a place of worship. This is erroneous. This house was contracted for in 1682, and the first meeting that was held in it was upon the 24th of the 8th month (Oct.) 1684, O. S. This building, one of the very oldest in the State, is well preserved, and though frequently enlarged and repaired, retains much of its original appearance and arrangement.

[2] The following is the text of the minutes of this meeting: "Att our "Men's Meeting att Wenlock Chrystisons ye 24th day of ye 1st month "1676 It was concluded by ye meeting yt ye meeting house at Betty's "Cove should be finished as followeth, vizt: To scale ye Gable end and "ye Loft with Clapboards, and make a partition betwixt ye new roome, "and ye old one, three foot high, seiled, and with windows to lift up and "down, and to be hung with hinges, according to ye direction of Bryan "O'Mealy, and John Pitt, who are appointed by the meeting to have ye "oversight of ye same, and to be done with what conveniency may be."

individuals, but there are other evidences that he held a station of honor and confidence in his society. It has been shown that his house was a place of meeting for Friends when business connected with the society was to be considered. In the year 1674, it appears that he was one of the petitioners to the General Assembly of Maryland for a modification of the law with regard to oaths, asking that Friends be allowed to make their solemn affirmation, instead of being required to swear, which, in their prayer for relief, they say "they dare not do." He was one of those appointed by the meetings to present this petition to the Governor and Council, and as his name heads the list, the text of this address, which is upon record, was probably from his pen. This paper was sent by the Upper to the Lower House, but some doubt arising as to the right of the General Assembly to alter the form of oath prescribed by the law of England, it was referred back again to the Upper House, which ordered it to remain upon the journal until the opinion of the Lord Proprietary could be obtained, who declared, when it was laid before him, that though he formerly had intentions of gratifying the desire of the Friends in this matter, he wished "all proceedings thereon to be for the present suspended," assigning no reason for this course. The object of this petition was not fully attained until the year 1702, when the "Act for the establishment of religious worship in this Province, according to the Church of England," was passed, upon which a section was engrafted declaring that "the solemn affirmation or declaration of the people called Quakers should be accepted, instead of an oath in the usual form." For so long a time were these good citizens liable to vexations and losses even in tolerant Maryland! But, while presenting this petition to the Governor and his Council, we see Wenlock Christison in a very different position from that he occupied when before Governor Endicott and the court in Massachusetts. The committee of the Friends' meeting, of which he was apparently the chairman or speaker, was received courteously by Governor Calvert, subsequently Lord Proprietary, and by his Council, and its complaint was respectfully considered. Let us indulge the fancy that Christison was allowed to wear his hat in the Governor's presence, a privilege so estimable that rather than forego it, he once had shown himself ready to be led to the gallows.[1]

[1] Although there was no Act of Assembly for the relief of Quakers and other dissenters until the date mentioned, there were English statutes for the relief of these people, which were operative in the colonies, and which were passed many years before. The provisions of these acts were only confirmed by the Colonial Act of 1702. But in the absence of legal, there was a popular tolerance, sustained, it is true, by these parliamentary enactments, that controlled the colonial government, and this popular tolerance secured to the Friends their rights and privileges almost as effectually as if the Assembly had passed ordinances for that purpose.

But Wenlock Christison did not enjoy the confidence of Friends only, for we have indubitable evidence of the respect and esteem in which he was held by the citizens of the county at large, in the fact that he was elected to the highly honorable place of Burgess or Delegate to the General Assembly of the province. Opportunity has not offered to determine the date of his election, but it is known that there was a proclamation of a general election made in April, 1676, and that Wenlock Christison is mentioned in 1681 as having been a member of the Lower House, but then dead. It is presumable that he was chosen in the former year, and held his seat until his death, which took place somewhere about 1679. He was probably the first Quaker who had occupied a political position in Talbot county. Friends were sent to the Assembly from other parts of the province. John Edmondson, the liberal friend of Christison, appears to have been elected September 2, 1681, to fill the place made vacant by his death, and he took his seat in the Assembly in November of that year.[1] Although Friends, by their scruples upon many matters with which government has to deal, have been, for the most part, debarred from political and civil position, it is certain that about the time of the events here related, they

---

[1] The authorities for these details are the State and county records.

were members of the Lower House of Assembly, as has just been shown, and they were also Justices of the Peace. In 1685 no less than three out of ten of the county Judges or Justices were Quakers, viz: William Sharpe, William Stevens, and Ralph Fishbourne. It would appear, from a minute of the meeting, that the election of Wenlock Christison and other Friends to the Assembly, did not give entire satisfaction, and that politicians, then as now, were ready to raise captious objections. It would seem that Col. Vincent Lowe, a conspicuous character of the county of Talbot, circulated a report "of Friends that were chosen Assembly men," the purport of which was that "Friends should be "the occasion of Leavyes (Levies or taxes) being "raised soe high." This report, of which nothing more is known, scandalized the Friends to that degree that the attention of the monthly meeting at Third Haven was at first called to it, and by that meeting it was referred to the yearly meeting. A committee was appointed on the 3rd of the 8th month (Oct. 14th) 1677, composed of John Edmondson, Bryan O'Mealy and Ralph Fishbourne, "to treat with Lowe, for ye clear-"ing of Friends and ye Truth," so solicitous were these people of avoiding all reproach. There is little doubt that Wenlock Christison's conduct as an "Assembly man" was the subject of Col.

Vincent Lowe's animadversions, and of this early committee's investigations.[1]

There is nothing in Bishope's Book to lead one to believe that Christison, while undergoing persecutions in New England, was a man of family. No reference is made to his having a wife or children: but among the very first notices of him in Maryland, namely, that made in the will of Peter Sharpe, already quoted, is one that speaks of him as being a married man. The devise is to "Wenlock Christison and his wife." But there are in the minutes of the meeting at Third Haven other references to this fact, some of which are exceedingly curious. The following needs no apology for its insertion here, being interesting and suggestive: "Att our "Man's meeting at Wenlock Christison's, ye 14th "of ye 5th month, 1676, Wenlock Christison "declared in ye meeting that if ye world, or "any particular person should speak evilly of "ye Truth, or reproach Friends concerning his "proceedings in taking his wife, that then he "will give further satisfaction and clear ye Truth "and Friends, by giving forth a paper to con- "demn his hasty and forward proceedings in yt "matter, and said that were ye thing to do "again he would not proceed so hasty, nor

---

[1] Minutes Friends' meeting at Third Haven, vol. 4.

"without consent of Friends."[1] It is very clear from this that Wenlock Christison had, then, recently married; that he had married either without having made the proper advertisement of his purpose in meeting, or he had married out of the society, some one not a member, for which he had been called to account. It is likely, therefore, this was a second marriage, for the Friends would certainly not have called him to an account in 1676 for a marriage contracted anterior to 1672—or at least four years before. So it appears that Wenlock Christison, prophet and apostle, and almost martyr, as he was, was not insensible to female charms, and that he whom the threats of judges and the whips of

[1] The assumption of the marriage relation gave much solicitude and trouble to the early Friends in Maryland, as elsewhere. Two causes are mentioned in the text for disquietude—the marriages out of the society of their members, and precipitate marriages without formal publication of the banns. Another source of annoyance, which was usually coupled with one or both the others, was the marriage of their children by Priests and magistrates. This will be referred to presently. The matter of obtaining the consent of the meeting to a marriage was neither arbitrary nor foolish It was a very necessary precaution at that day and under the circumstances. It was intended, or at least it was a part of the intention of this custom, to prevent the connubial union of persons who already had husbands or wives in the old country. It was not unusual, upon the publication in meeting of proposed marriages, to appoint a committee of Friends to inquire as to the "freedom" of the parties, or whether they were "clear." Too many of the emigrants to Maryland had deserted their lawful partners, and, after a short residence here, were ready to take others. The Friends took every precaution to prevent such a scandal from being fastened upon any whom they could control, by ordering an investigation of their relations at home in the old country, or in the neighboring provinces.

constables could not subdue, yielded to the blandishments of a fair lady, so far as to forget, not the requirements of rectitude, to be sure, but the exactions of ecclesiastical rule. There was, on his part, no lapse from virtue nor fall from grace, but only a little obliviousness of *canonical* law, more readily pardoned by the world than by the church authorities, even though those authorities be Friends, who have ever been very indulgent to the infirmities of human nature, when the "Truth" was not compromised thereby.

That children were born to Wenlock Christison is well attested. His eldest daugther Mary married one John Dine, who lived upon St. Michæl's river, but subsequently moved to Kent Island, where he may have representatives to this day. It is thought another daughter married Peter Harrod, or more properly, Harwood, a leading Friend, who lived and died in Talbot. An Elizabeth Christison is mentioned in the rent rolls of the Lord Proprietary, as being taxed upon lands, as late as 1755. This may have been another daughter, or grand daughter. Of the marriage of one of his daughters, a very curious account is given in the minutes of the Third Haven meeting, held the 5th. day of the 12th month $169\frac{2}{3}$, O. S., which, as it illustrates some of the customs of the early Friends, may here be fully given. It must be premised that William Dixon, who is mentioned in this minute, married the widow of Wenlock Christison, and hence he may, according to an erroneous usage, have called a daughter of his wife a daughter-in-law. William Dixon certainly had no children of his own. The following is the entry in the minutes: "William Dixon informs this meeting "yt his Daughter-in-law is stole away and mar- "ried by a priest in ye night, contrary to his "and his wife's minds; that he has opposed the "same, and refused to pay her portion, for which "he is cited to appear before ye Comissary gen- "eralle, and now he desires to know whether "ye meeting would stand by him, if he should "sue ye priest yt married her. Ye meeting "assents to it, and promises to stand by him "in it, he taking ye meeting's advice from time "to time in his proceedings therein."

Nothing seems to have afflicted Friends in Talbot more than the "outgoings" of members of the society in marriage. To be married with a license, by a magistrate, or by a "hireling priest,"[1] was an abomination in their eyes, the could not go unreproved. At a meeting held the 24th of the 4th month (July 1st), 1681, the

[1] The Rev. Mr. Lillingston, one of the earliest of the ministers of the Church of England, in Talbot, who lived in the upper part of the county, was particularly obnoxious on account of his frequent services to impatient young Quakers.

committee that was appointed to wait on the Lord Proprietary "concerning Friends' children "being taken away from them and married "by the priest without their consent or know- "ledge," gave an answer to the effect that they were treated "very civilly" by the Proprietary, who said, among other things, "that for ye "future he would take care in all his counties "that the like should be prevented." The evil continuing unabated, the quarterly meeting held 10th of 6th mo. (Aug. 21st), 1688, recommended that Friends should disinherit their disobedient children, and give them "no part nor parcel of their outward substance." This action of the quarterly was confirmed by the yearly meeting held at Third Haven the 9th of the 8th. month, (Oct. 20th), 1688, with a supplementary recommen- dation that "priests or magistrates that do marry "Friends' children without their parents or guar- "dians consent, should be prosecuted." This explains the conduct of William Dixon in his appeal to the meeting to "stand by him" in his refusal to pay over the portion due to a daugh- ter of Wenlock Christison (probably), and in his proposal to sue the priest who married her. History is silent as to the names of the offend- ers. William Dixon died without heirs of his body, leaving the estate derived, in part, through his marriage with Elizabeth, the widow of Wenlock Christison, to Isaac Dixon, the son of a brother, he having first bought out the interest of Mary Christison Dine in 1684. This account of the proceedings relating to the marriage of one who is reasonably supposed to have been Christison's daughter, furnishes evidences of the extreme liberality of sentiment that prevailed towards the Friends in Maryland: more than this, it shows that there was a disposition to indulge them to an extent which would not be tolerated in the present day. No countenance would now be given by the people of this State, nor by the courts, to an attempt to deprive a ward of her property because she had married a man not of her religious society, or had been married by a clergyman of some other religious denomination than her own. Much less would they countenance a suit for damages against a clergyman so offending a mere religious prejudice, even though that prejudice had acquired the dignity of ecclesiastical rule. It is hardly necessary to say these rules of the meeting are neither followed nor approved by the society of Friends of the present day, who are not of those who think a custom is good because it is old, or a doctrine true because it is ancient.

The precise date of Wenlock Christison's death is nowhere given, and unfortunately his will, to which reference has been made more than once, is to be found neither in the county records nor in the minutes of the Third Haven meeting. It is, however, pretty certain that he died about 1678 or 1679, and it is very certain that he made a will appointing his wife Elizabeth executrix, jointly with William Sharpe and Thomas Taylor. In 1679 it is stated in the minutes that she was about to marry again, and the meeting took measures to have her late husband's estate properly partitioned to the heirs and legatees. John Edmondson, Bryan O'Mealy and William Southbee were appointed by the meeting, in accordance with an early custom of Friends, to counsel, advise and assist the executrix in the settlement of the estate. It is worthy of note, in this connection, that the early Friends in Maryland took especial care of the interests of orphans, and protected their estates by other than legal guards. They even had a register for the society whose duty it was to preserve a record of wills, at a time when there *seems* to have been no official registration, or at a time when such registration, if made, was at a distant point. By his will Wenlock Christison set free his faithful servant John Stacy, the same whom, as mentioned above, he carried into court to have the Justices determine how long he should serve his master.

Where Wenlock Christison was buried is not known, but probably at the meeting house at Betty's Cove, to which there was a burial ground attached, now long obliterated. No monumental stone marks the grave of this worthy, for "the people called Quakers" will not minister to a vanity that seeks posthumous display by erecting memorials to their dead, nor gratify the pride or affection of the living by blazoning on their tombs, in false or fulsome praise, the virtues of departed Friends. They who look with such confidence to an immortality beyond the grave, are not apt to be solicitous for that transitory fame the most glowing epitaphs upon perishable marble bestow; and they build no shrines, to which pious pilgrimages may be made, over the relics of their saints. So Wenlock Christison sleeps in an undistinguished tomb, and yet he is more secure of a lasting memory than if his resting place was marked by "storied urn or animated bust," for his labors and sufferings in the cause of "Light and Life," are imperishably engraved upon the minds and hearts of Friends throughout the world, while his courage, his firmness and his constancy are and shall ever be the themes of the historians of his country.

Here properly should terminate this memoir, but an occurrence that happened after his death reveals an incident in the life of this Quaker worthy, so strange and startling that, although the absence of date has prevented its incorporation in this essay in its chronological position, it must not be omitted. It will be recollected it was stated that there is sufficient evidence on record to render it probable that Wenlock Christison, after leaving New England, sometime between the years 1665 and 1670, went to Barbadoes; also, in another place, that he had possession, after settling in Talbot, of African slaves, as well as European indentured servants. Now this evidence is furnished by a brief minute of the Third Haven meeting, under date of 16th. of 7th month (Sept. 27th), 1681. This minute is to the effect that the executors of his last will and testament, namely, Elizabeth his wife, William Sharpe and Thomas Taylor, had been arrested at the suit of "one Diggs, concerning of "some negroes sent by Wenlock Christison "out of Barbadoes to this country." Not improbably this Diggs was that Col. Diggs who, at one time, was a Justice of the Provincial Court and member of the Upper House of Assembly, and who commanded at St. Mary's when the archives of the province were surrendered to John Coode, the leader of the forces of the Protestant Association, at the time of the revolution in 1689. The phraseology of the minutes would seem to indicate that these negroes were not purchased from a cargo imported by Col. Diggs, but that they were *sent* by Christison out of Barbadoes, he himself being present in the islands, and making the shipment on his own account.

It is well known that the West India islands were depôts for the reception of slaves brought from the coast of Africa, and that from the barracoons upon these islands they were sold to shippers trading with the various colonies. The Quakers have been so long, and they were such early opponents of the whole system of slavery, that many suppose that their "testimony" has always been against the holding of man in bondage. This is of course erroneous. Well informed Friends know that negro slaves were held by the early members of the society—indeed were held, in gradually decreasing numbers, down to a comparatively recent date. The records of their meetings here, as well as the records of the court of Talbot county, indicate this fact, and it is mentioned by their historians. The glory of the society is, that at so early a period, even before the public conscience had been awakened, and at a time when the pecuniary interests of its members were so heavily involved—interests which have so much to do with our moral decisions—it should have uttered, first its advice, and then its command, against the holding of slaves.[1] But before advice had been given by the meetings, there had grown up a sensitiveness in the minds of individual members of the society on this subject.[2] Thus, William Dixon, in the year 1684, (according to the minutes of Third Haven meeting,) wishing "to sell a negro his freedom desires ye meeting's advice." No advice is given, but he is referred to the yearly meeting "for advice in yt particular." This same William Dixon, he who married the widow of Wenlock Christison, by his will, admitted to probate in 1708, emancipated several negroes and made provision for their support by

[1] In the year 1759 the yearly meeting of Maryland advises care in importing and buying negroes, but does not condemn. In 1760 the meeting condemns importing slaves. In 1762 the meeting condemns importing and buying, and also selling without the consent of the meeting. In 1777 slaveholding was made the ground of "disownment."

[2] The growth of the sentiment of condemnation of slavery in Maryland, with its increase at one period and its decline at another, until it reached its present *status*, would furnish a most interesting and instructive chapter in the history of morals. The influence of Quakerism upon this growth, in such an account, could not be omitted.

It is a most curious fact which may be mentioned here, though somewhat out of place, that it was deemed necessary to pass a law in Maryland for the purpose of quieting the consciences and titles of the scrupulous slave-holders, to this effect: "That no negro or negroes, by receiving "the Holy Sacrament of Baptism, is thereby manumitted or set free, nor "hath any right or title to freedom or manumission, more than he or they "had before; any law, usage or custom to the contrary notwithstanding." This was done for the sake of those who, having been defending African slavery upon the ground of its introducing heathens into Christianity, saw the illogicalness of their position when these slaves were admitted to baptism, and therefore refused to allow them to observe that rite.

Bacon's Laws, 1715, *chap.* XLIV, *sec.* XXIV.

giving them land and means to build houses. In his will he says they had served him twenty years. There can be little doubt that some of these people, whom he felt called upon to set free, were of that cargo of negroes sent out of Barbadoes by Wenlock Christison, for the recovery of the value of which suit was brought by Col. Diggs. Even so early then as the dates here given, there was evidently a repugnance upon the part of Friends to holding slaves. The subject of the growth of the sentiment of hostility to slavery among this people is one of the most interesting that can engage the attention of the ethical philosopher; and its study may serve to elucidate, if not solve, that great problem which has bothered the brains of students of the human mind for thousands of years, the origin of our notions of right and wrong. Those who believe that there has been enthroned in every man's bosom a severe and incorruptible arbiter who passes upon the moral quality of every action with infallible rectitude of decision, will hesitate and doubt when viewing this case of Wenlock Christison. Here was a man whose fundamental religious belief was, the presence in his own bosom, and in the bosoms of all "Friends of Truth," of an inspired monitor that warned him of evil and prompted him to the good only; a man belonging to a society whose pure and lofty code of morals has been the admiration of the ages, but to the standard of which those ages have never yet attained; a man so firm and tenacious of what he deemed the right, that sooner than bate one jot or tittle—sooner than even take off his hat in honor of man, or hold up his hand except in prayer—was prepared to go to the gallows, and who did actually receive many cruel and ignominious scourgings; a man who had manifested in his life a readiness to follow the Light which he verily believed was divinely enlightening him, even though the following it should lead him into the very jaws of death; a man whose loftiness of purpose and sanctity of life had been such that partial Friends had attributed to him the inspiration of the prophet and the miraculous power of the apostle,—here was a man who, without compunction, with entire innocence, as we may be well assured, could, and did, deliberately engage in a transaction which at this day, by the common consent of humanity and religion, of reason and sentiment, possesses every element of injustice and impiety. That Friends, in the moral twilight of two hundred years ago, should have held the slaves they had inherited from their parents, acquired by marriage with their wives, or even purchased from traders before they had been " convinced "— before the " inner light " had dawned upon their minds—we might be prepared to believe: but that a Friend should have been among the very first of whom there is any account in this county of Talbot, to participate in the slave trade, and that this Friend should have been Wenlock Christison, is so incredible that it would be beyond belief if it were not so well attested. In our judgments of men, so astounding a fact as this "must give us pause."

www.ingramcontent.com/pod-product-compliance
Lightning Source LLC
Chambersburg PA
CBHW020232090426
42735CB00010B/1657